At Issue

Are Newspapers Becoming Extinct?

Other Books in the At Issue Series:

At Issue

Are Newspapers Becoming Extinct?

Jennifer Dorman, Book Editor

GREENHAVEN PRESS
A part of Gale, Cengage Learning

Detroit • New York • San Francisco • New Haven, Conn • Waterville, Maine • London

GALE
CENGAGE Learning™

Christine Nasso, *Publisher*
Elizabeth Des Chenes, *Managing Editor*

© 2011 Greenhaven Press, a part of Gale, Cengage Learning.

Gale and Greenhaven Press are registered trademarks used herein under license.

For more information, contact:
Greenhaven Press
27500 Drake Rd.
Farmington Hills, MI 48331-3535
Or you can visit our Internet site at gale.cengage.com

For product information and technology assistance, contact us at

Gale Customer Support, 1-800-877-4253
For permission to use material from this text or product, submit all requests online at
www.cengage.com/permissions

Further permissions questions can be e-mailed to permissionrequest@cengage.com

Articles in Greenhaven Press anthologies are often edited for length to meet page require-ments. In addition, original titles of these works are changed to clearly present the main thesis and to explicitly indicate the author's opinion. Every effort is made to ensure that Greenhaven Press accurately reflects the original intent of the authors. Every effort has been made to trace the owners of copyrighted material.

Cover photograph reproduced by permission of Brand X Pictures.

LIBRARY OF CONGRESS CATALOGING-IN-PUBLICATION DATA

Are newspapers becoming extinct? / Jennifer Dorman, book editor.
p. cm. -- (At issue)
Includes bibliographical references and index.
ISBN 978-0-7377-5143-7 (hardcover) -- ISBN 978-0-7377-5144-4 (pbk.)
1. Newspaper publishing--Forecasting. 2. Technological innovations. I. Dorman, Jennifer.
PN4734.A74 2011
070.5'722--dc22
2011005913

Printed in the United States of America
1 2 3 4 5 6 7 15 14 13 12 11

Contents

Introduction

On May 24, 2010, the Federal Trade Commission (FTC) released a controversial "discussion draft" titled "Potential Policy Recommendations to Support the Reinvention of Journalism." The document states that "newspapers have not yet found a new sustainable business model, and there is reason for concern that such a business model may not emerge."[1] The paper, which lists potential policy proposals, was meant as fodder for a final workshop on the subject as well as to encourage a national conversation. The proposals were compiled from two earlier FTC workshops, where participants ranged from news business leaders and journalists to new media entrepreneurs and bloggers. Ideas were also gleaned from reports, articles, and Senate hearings on the future of journalism.

Among the proposals were various legislative measures that might prevent online aggregational news sites, such as the *Drudge Report* and *Google*, from undermining newspaper revenue. Other ideas included taxing consumer electronics, subsidizing journalists' salaries, starting a journalism branch of AmeriCorps, and establishing citizenship news vouchers whereby individuals could designate a portion of their taxes to a news organization of their choice.

Although these were not official recommendations, the FTC still encountered widespread criticism for the document. The impulse to "save journalism" strikes many people as a desire to prop up the dying business model of an old institution. In an opinion piece for the *New York Post*, Jeffrey Jarvis writes:

> I believe [the] future is entrepreneurial, not institutional. . . .
> But those entrepreneurs don't need government help. They
> need to be left alone with the assurance they won't be inter-
> fered with by the FTC—or the FCC [Federal Communi-

cations Commission], which has its own hearings and reports on the future of journalism.[2]

While the belief that the free market will find a way to support journalism is widely held, proponents of public policies that support media see journalism suffering at the hands of the market.

In a presentation for the FTC workshops, Robert McChesney, cofounder of the media reform organization Free Press, talked about journalism as a public good, "something society requires, and people want, but the market cannot generate in sufficient quantity or quality. It requires government leadership to exist."[3] He added that "the public-good nature of journalism was masked for the past century by the emergence of advertising to provide anywhere from 60–100 percent of the revenues for major news media."

Critics of intervention, such as Mark Tapscott of *The Washington Examiner,* take issue with the notion of a "public good" that is "defined and regulated by the government."[4] Likewise, the idea that the government would be involved in the very mechanism meant to keep it accountable strikes many as an affront to democracy. In response to the FTC's discussion draft, a *Washington Times* editorial outlined the pitfalls for a free press (also known as the Fourth Estate) inherent in this approach:

> The conflict of interest in having the government pay or contribute to a newsman's salary could not be more obvious. Reporters and columnists would have little incentive to offer critical analyses of tax increases that might mean a boost in the pocketbook.[5]

Whether journalism can remain independent if supported and regulated by government is no small question. The editorial continues with a dire prediction that "each year at budget time, the Fourth Estate would scramble to be worthy in the eyes of Capitol Hill for increased support."

Amid the outcry that government involvement undermines democracy, it is important to note that the US government has a long history of involvement with the media, including discounted newspaper delivery dating back to the Postal Act of 1792, as well as tax subsidies and the Public Broadcasting Act of 1967, which established the Corporation for Public Broadcasting. Josh Stearnes of the blog SaveThe News.org writes that "government has always and will always influence how our media system is shaped. The question is not 'if,' it is 'how.'"[6] Stearnes continues:

> When many of the smartest minds working on the future of journalism promote the notion that the government should just "Get off our lawn," they take themselves (and many others) out of the debate, leaving it up to the corporate lobbyists in Washington DC to decide what the future of journalism will be.

Historically, the government's role in the news industry has met with a vocal, though relatively minor, protest. The outcry that followed the FTC proposal indicates that increased government involvement might lead to far greater disapproval.

The expressed purpose of the discussion draft was to generate debate, and this it certainly did. According to Susan De-Santi of the FTC, there may not be any recommendations that come out of this exploration because, she notes, "we're in the midst of a profound transition in the news. Nobody knows exactly where this is going to end up, and nobody really knows at what point we are in this transition."[7]

While no policy recommendations have emerged from the FTC's discussion draft, the discussion is ongoing. Well beyond the issue of government involvement, the state of the news media is a subject that is simultaneously being mourned, celebrated, debated, and anticipated. *At Issue: Are Newspapers Becoming Extinct?* explores a variety of viewpoints debating the options for traditional media, the value of new media, and the importance of journalism.

Notes

1. Federal Trade Commission Staff Discussion Draft: Potential Policy Recommendations to Support the Reinvention of Journalism.
2. Jeffrey Jarvis, "How Not to Save News: Bad Gov't Ideas for Journalism," *New York Post*, June 3, 2010.
3. Robert McChesney, "Rejuvenating American Journalism: Some Tentative Policy Proposals," Presentation to the Workshop on Journalism, Federal Trade Commission, March 10, 2010.
4. Mark Tapscott, "Will Journalists Wake Up in Time to Save Journalism from Obama's FTC?" *Washington Examiner*, May 29, 2010.
5. *Washington Times*, editorial, June 4, 2010.
6. Josh Stearnes, SaveTheNews.org, June 2, 2010. www.savethe news.org.
7. Quoted in Jeremy W. Peters, "Government Takes on Journalism's Next Chapter," *New York Times*, June 13, 2010.

1

Traditional Newspapers Are Becoming Extinct

Clay Shirky

Clay Shirky is an associate teacher at New York University's Interactive Telecommunications Program. He publishes the monthly newsletter Networks, Economics, and Culture.

The newspaper industry has been fighting for its life since the beginning of the digital age. All of the plans and arguments developed by print media advocates fail to acknowledge that the advent of the Internet heralded the inevitable demise of newspapers. We are living through a revolution much like the one that accompanied the invention of the printing press. Journalism will survive without newspapers, but there is no way for us to know now what the next phase of journalism will look like.

Back in 1993, the Knight-Ridder newspaper chain began investigating piracy of Dave Barry's popular column, which was published by the *Miami Herald* and syndicated widely. In the course of tracking down the sources of unlicensed distribution, they found many things, including the copying of his column to alt.fan.dave_barry on usenet; a 2000-person-strong mailing list also reading pirated versions; and a teenager in the Midwest who was doing some of the copying himself, because he loved Barry's work so much he wanted everybody to be able to read it.

One of the people I was hanging around with online back then was Gordy Thompson, who managed internet services at

Clay Shirky, "Newspapers and Thinking the Unthinkable," www.shirky.com, March 13, 2009. Reprinted with permission.

the *New York Times*. I remember Thompson saying something to the effect of "When a 14-year-old kid can blow up your business in his spare time, not because he hates you but because he loves you, then you got a problem." I think about that conversation a lot these days.

Strategizing to Survive the Internet

The problem newspapers face isn't that they didn't see the internet coming. They not only saw it miles off, they figured out early on that they needed a plan to deal with it, and during the early 90s they came up with not just one plan but several. One was to partner with companies like America Online, a fast-growing subscription service that was less chaotic than the open internet. Another plan was to educate the public about the behaviors required of them by copyright law. New payment models such as micropayments were proposed. Alternatively, they could pursue the profit margins enjoyed by radio and TV, if they became purely ad-supported. Still another plan was to convince tech firms to make their hardware and software less capable of sharing, or to partner with the businesses running data networks to achieve the same goal. Then there was the nuclear option: sue copyright infringers directly, making an example of them.

> The problem newspapers face isn't that they didn't see the internet coming.

As these ideas were articulated, there was intense debate about the merits of various scenarios. Would DRM [digital rights management] or walled gardens work better? Shouldn't we try a carrot-and-stick approach, with education *and* prosecution? And so on. In all this conversation, there was one scenario that was widely regarded as unthinkable, a scenario that didn't get much discussion in the nation's newsrooms, for the obvious reason.

Ignoring Reality

The unthinkable scenario unfolded something like this: The ability to share content wouldn't shrink, it would grow. Walled gardens would prove unpopular. Digital advertising would reduce inefficiencies, and therefore profits. Dislike of micropayments would prevent widespread use. People would resist being educated to act against their own desires. Old habits of advertisers and readers would not transfer online. Even ferocious litigation would be inadequate to constrain massive, sustained law-breaking. (Prohibition redux.) Hardware and software vendors would not regard copyright holders as allies, nor would they regard customers as enemies. DRM's requirement that the attacker be allowed to decode the content would be an insuperable flaw. And, per Thompson, suing people who love something so much they want to share it would piss them off.

Revolutions create a curious inversion of perception. In ordinary times, people who do no more than describe the world around them are seen as pragmatists, while those who imagine fabulous alternative futures are viewed as radicals. The last couple of decades haven't been ordinary, however. Inside the papers, the pragmatists were the ones simply looking out the window and noticing that the real world increasingly resembled the unthinkable scenario. These people were treated as if they were barking mad. Meanwhile the people spinning visions of popular walled gardens and enthusiastic micropayment adoption, visions unsupported by reality, were regarded not as charlatans but saviors.

When reality is labeled unthinkable, it creates a kind of sickness in an industry. Leadership becomes faith-based, while employees who have the temerity to suggest that what seems to be happening is in fact happening are herded into Innovation Departments, where they can be ignored *en bloc* [as a unit]. This shunting aside of the realists in favor of the fabulists has different effects on different industries at different times. One of the effects on the newspapers is that many of their most passionate defenders are unable, even now, to plan for a world in which the industry they knew is visibly going away.

When someone demands to know how we are going to replace newspapers, they are really demanding to be told that we are not living through a revolution.

Traditional Publishing Is Irrelevant

The curious thing about the various plans hatched in the '90s is that they were, at base, all the same plan: "Here's how we're going to preserve the old forms of organization in a world of cheap perfect copies!" The details differed, but the core assumption behind all imagined outcomes (save the unthinkable one) was that the organizational form of the newspaper, as a general-purpose vehicle for publishing a variety of news and opinion, was basically sound, and only needed a digital facelift. As a result, the conversation has degenerated into the enthusiastic grasping at straws, pursued by skeptical responses.

"The *Wall Street Journal* has a paywall, so we can too!" (Financial information is one of the few kinds of information whose recipients don't want to share.) "Micropayments work for iTunes, so they will work for us!" (Micropayments work only where the provider can avoid competitive business models.) "The *New York Times* should charge for content!" (They've tried, with QPass and later TimesSelect.) "Cook's Illustrated and Consumer Reports are doing fine on subscriptions!" (Those publications forgo ad revenues; users are paying not just for content but for unimpeachability.) "We'll form a cartel!" (. . . and hand a competitive advantage to every ad-supported media firm in the world.)

Round and round this goes, with the people committed to saving newspapers demanding to know "If the old model is broken, what will work in its place?" To which the answer is: Nothing. Nothing will work. There is no general model for newspapers to replace the one the internet just broke.

With the old economics destroyed, organizational forms perfected for industrial production have to be replaced with structures optimized for digital data. It makes increasingly less sense even to talk about a publishing industry, because the core problem publishing solves—the incredible difficulty, complexity, and expense of making something available to the public—has stopped being a problem.

The Printing Press Revolution

Elizabeth Eisenstein's magisterial treatment of [Johannes] Gutenberg's invention [of the printing press] *The Printing Press as an Agent of Change*, opens with a recounting of her research into the early history of the printing press. She was able to find many descriptions of life in the early 1400s, the era before movable type. Literacy was limited, the Catholic Church was the pan-European political force, Mass was in Latin, and the average book was the Bible. She was also able to find endless descriptions of life in the late 1500s, after Gutenberg's invention had started to spread. Literacy was on the rise, as were books written in contemporary languages, [Nicolaus] Copernicus had published his epochal work on astronomy, and Martin Luther's use of the press to reform the Church was upending both religious and political stability.

What Eisenstein focused on, though, was how many historians ignored the transition from one era to the other. To describe the world before or after the spread of print was child's play; those dates were safely distanced from upheaval. But what was happening in 1500? The hard question Eisenstein's book asks is "How did we get from the world before the printing press to the world after it? What was the revolution *itself* like?"

Chaotic, as it turns out. The Bible was translated into local languages; was this an educational boon or the work of the devil? Erotic novels appeared, prompting the same set of questions. Copies of [ancient Greek philosopher] Aristotle and [ancient Greek physician] Galen circulated widely, but direct encounter with the relevant texts revealed that the two sources clashed, tarnishing faith in the Ancients. As novelty spread, old institutions seemed exhausted while new ones seemed untrustworthy; as a result, people almost literally didn't know what to think. If you can't trust Aristotle, who can you trust?

During the wrenching transition to print, experiments were only revealed in retrospect to be turning points. Aldus Manutius, the Venetian printer and publisher, invented the smaller *octavo* volume along with italic type. What seemed like a minor change—take a book and shrink it—was in retrospect a key innovation in the democratization of the printed word. As books became cheaper, more portable, and therefore more desirable, they expanded the market for all publishers, heightening the value of literacy still further.

A New Revolution

That is what real revolutions are like. The old stuff gets broken faster than the new stuff is put in its place. The importance of any given experiment isn't apparent at the moment it appears; big changes stall, small changes spread. Even the revolutionaries can't predict what will happen. Agreements on all sides that core institutions must be protected are rendered meaningless by the very people doing the agreeing. (Luther and the Church both insisted, for years, that whatever else happened, no one was talking about a schism.) Ancient social bargains, once disrupted, can neither be mended nor quickly replaced, since any such bargain takes decades to solidify.

And so it is today. When someone demands to know how we are going to replace newspapers, they are really demanding to be told that we are not living through a revolution. They are demanding to be told that old systems won't break before new systems are in place. They are demanding to be told that ancient social bargains aren't in peril, that core institutions will be spared, that new methods of spreading information will improve previous practice rather than upending it. They are demanding to be lied to.

"You're gonna miss us when we're gone!" has never been much of a business model.

There are fewer and fewer people who can convincingly tell such a lie.

Newspaper Economics

If you want to know why newspapers are in such trouble, the most salient fact is this: Printing presses are terrifically expensive to set up and to run. This bit of economics, normal since Gutenberg, limits competition while creating positive returns to scale for the press owner, a happy pair of economic effects that feed on each other. In a notional [theoretical] town with two perfectly balanced newspapers, one paper would eventually generate some small advantage—a breaking story, a key interview—at which point both advertisers and readers would come to prefer it, however slightly. That paper would in turn find it easier to capture the next dollar of advertising, at lower expense, than the competition. This would increase its dominance, which would further deepen those preferences, repeat chorus. The end result is either geographic or demographic segmentation among papers, or one paper holding a monopoly on the local mainstream audience.

For a long time, longer than anyone in the newspaper business has been alive in fact, print journalism has been intertwined with these economics. The expense of printing created an environment where Wal-Mart was willing to subsidize the Baghdad bureau. This wasn't because of any deep link between advertising and reporting, nor was it about any real desire on the part of Wal-Mart to have their marketing budget go to international correspondents. It was just an accident. Advertisers had little choice other than to have their money used that way, since they didn't really have any other vehicle for display ads.

The old difficulties and costs of printing forced everyone doing it into a similar set of organizational models; it was this similarity that made us regard *Daily Racing Form* and *L'Osservatore Romano* as being in the same business. That the relationship between advertisers, publishers, and journalists has been ratified by a century of cultural practice doesn't make it any less accidental.

Experiments are only revealed in retrospect to be turning points.

The competition-deflecting effects of printing cost got destroyed by the internet, where everyone pays for the infrastructure, and then everyone gets to use it. And when Wal-Mart, and the local Maytag dealer, and the law firm hiring a secretary, and that kid down the block selling his bike, were all able to use that infrastructure to get out of their old relationship with the publisher, they did. They'd never really signed up to fund the Baghdad bureau anyway.

An Unpredictable Future

Print media does much of society's heavy journalistic lifting, from flooding the zone—covering every angle of a huge story—to the daily grind of attending the City Council meeting, just in case. This coverage creates benefits even for people who aren't newspaper readers, because the work of print journalists is used by everyone from politicians to district attorneys to talk radio hosts to bloggers. The newspaper people often note that newspapers benefit society as a whole. This is true, but irrelevant to the problem at hand; "You're gonna miss us when we're gone!" has never been much of a business model. So who covers all that news if some significant fraction of the currently employed newspaper people lose their jobs?

I don't know. Nobody knows. We're collectively living through 1500, when it's easier to see what's broken than what will replace it. The internet turns 40 this fall [2009]. Access by the general public is less than half that age. Web use, as a normal part of life for a majority of the developed world, is less than half *that* age. We just got here. Even the revolutionaries can't predict what will happen.

Time to Experiment

Imagine, in 1996, asking some net-savvy soul to expound on the potential of craigslist, then a year old and not yet incorporated. The answer you'd almost certainly have gotten would be extrapolation: "Mailing lists can be powerful tools," "Social effects are intertwining with digital networks," blah blah blah. What no one would have told you, could have told you, was what actually happened: craigslist became a critical piece of infrastructure. Not the idea of craigslist, or the business model, or even the software driving it. Craigslist itself spread to cover hundreds of cities and has become a part of public consciousness about what is now possible. Experiments are only revealed in retrospect to be turning points.

Society doesn't need newspapers. What we need is journalism.

In craigslist's gradual shift from 'interesting if minor' to 'essential and transformative', there is one possible answer to the question "If the old model is broken, what will work in its place?" The answer is: Nothing will work, but everything might. Now is the time for experiments, lots and lots of experiments, each of which will seem as minor at launch as craigslist did, as Wikipedia did, as *octavo* volumes did.

Journalism Not Inextricably Bound to Newspapers

Journalism has always been subsidized. Sometimes it's been Wal-Mart and the kid with the bike. Sometimes it's been [politically conservative news media owner] Richard Mellon Scaife. Increasingly, it's you and me, donating our time. The list of models that are obviously working today, like *Consumer Reports* and NPR [National Public Radio] like ProPublica [left-leaning, nonprofit news organization] and WikiLeaks [an international news organization that promises a high level of security to anonymous sources], can't be expanded to cover any general case, but then nothing is going to cover the general case.

Society doesn't need newspapers. What we need is journalism. For a century, the imperatives to strengthen journalism and to strengthen newspapers have been so tightly wound as to be indistinguishable. That's been a fine accident to have, but when that accident stops, as it is stopping before our eyes, we're going to need lots of other ways to strengthen journalism instead.

When we shift our attention from 'save newspapers' to 'save society' the imperative changes from 'preserve the current institutions' to 'do whatever works.' And what works today isn't the same as what used to work.

A New Journalism Will Emerge

We don't know who the Aldus Manutius of the current age is. It could be [craigslist founder] Craig Newmark, or [Internet entrepreneur] Caterina Fake. It could be [vice president of digital operations for the New York Times Corporation] Martin Nisenholtz, or [director of digital content for the Guardian News Media] Emily Bell. It could be some 19 year old kid few of us have heard of, working on something we won't recognize as vital until a decade hence. Any experiment, though, designed to provide new models for journalism is going to be an improvement over hiding from the real, especially in a year when, for many papers, the unthinkable future is already in the past.

For the next few decades, journalism will be made up of overlapping special cases. Many of these models will rely on amateurs as researchers and writers. Many of these models will rely on sponsorship or grants or endowments instead of revenues. Many of these models will rely on excitable 14 year olds distributing the results. Many of these models will fail. No one experiment is going to replace what we are now losing with the demise of news on paper, but over time, the collection of new experiments that do work might give us the journalism we need.

2

Newspapers Will Not Become Extinct

Donna Barrett and Randy Siegel

Donna Barrett is president and chief executive of Community Newspaper Holdings Inc. and president of the Southern Newspaper Publishers Association. Randy Siegel is president and publisher of Parade Publications.

To be sure, newspapers are facing huge obstacles, but these challenges are not insurmountable. Current financial issues have much to do with the current recession, which is affecting every industry. Far from a death knell, digital media are creating new opportunities for news delivery and business innovation. Learning to better understand today's news audience, working to protect content, and communicating the value of quality journalism as well as print advertising will all help the newspaper industry to survive its current setbacks.

O kay, newspaper folks. It's time to pick ourselves off the ground and fight back. There is plenty of time left on the clock, and our fans—more than 100 million loyal readers in the United States—are pulling for us to win. So here's how we rally.

First and foremost, we have to ignore those self-proclaimed pundits and cynics who believe that newspapers are dead. They are dead wrong. Sure, newspaper companies face serious challenges. But we also have serious opportunities to reengineer ourselves as quality content creators for local print and online audiences that advertisers still desire.

As we are seeing during this punishing recession, overhauling the economics of newspapering while experimenting with new business models is a daunting task, but it's starting to happen in cities and towns all over America, especially where executives and editors possess the requisite vision, confidence, creativity and entrepreneurial drive to succeed.

Fortunately, the economy eventually will improve, and businesses will start spending more, even on newspaper ads.

The truth is that right now every media company is hurting and under tremendous pressure to innovate and grow, including Google, Yahoo, Microsoft, the broadcast networks, cable giants and radio conglomerates. No one—not even MySpace, Facebook or the latest new media darling—is immune from these severe contractions in the advertising marketplace. Newspapers may publish article after article about the problems they are experiencing, but they are not suffering alone.

Fortunately, the economy eventually will improve, and businesses will start spending more, even on newspaper ads. The price of newsprint will come down. New print and online revenue models will emerge. Organizational efficiencies will help the bottom line. And well-run newspaper companies will succeed by fighting hard, experimenting and evolving while tuning out those armchair critics who revel in the thought of a society without newspapers or news.

Second, newspaper companies need to capitalize more aggressively on the valuable information that their newsrooms singularly provide their communities and our country. In these uncertain, complex times, trusted, compelling content has the potential to be more essential for readers and online users than ever.

And if you don't believe us, ask yourself: Do most Americans still care about what goes on in their community, in their country and around the world? Is there still consumer demand for in-depth news, analysis, opinions, sports results and cultural coverage? Are the sharply shrunken TV and radio news operations in local markets really able to compete with the journalistic resources of a good newspaper? Are people looking for credible sources of news as it becomes increasingly difficult to separate fact from fiction on the Internet?

In the past year, newspaper journalists have blown away their competition with critically important and defining coverage of two wars, a historic presidential election and the worst economic meltdown and financial scandals in our lifetimes. In municipalities from coast to coast, newspapers have excelled in their watchdog role as a protector of the public interest by bringing down corrupt politicians, exposing government waste and fraud, and injecting much-needed accountability in our schools and social-service agencies.

In short, quality content is still king, and newspapers own the best news-gathering operations in their individual markets. Nearly all local news originates from newspaper journalists, which remains a huge competitive advantage if used the right way.

Are people looking for credible sources of news as it becomes increasingly difficult to separate fact from fiction on the Internet?

Newspapers can increase their revenues and reach by investing in more content creation for different audiences, not less. The more compelling articles and information a newspaper and its Web site can offer, the longer readers and online users will be engaged. The longer that consumers are engaged, the more exposure they will have to ads in print and online.

The more attention the ads receive, the better the advertisers' responses typically will be and the more those ads will be worth.

Bottom line: Creating a more attractive experience for newspaper and Web site audiences enhances advertising revenues. Conversely, cutting back too much on content while raising prices to readers and advertisers accelerates audience declines, which in turn undermine advertising revenues. It's pretty much impossible for any business, including newspapers, to increase market share and profitability by decreasing the quality of its product and driving away customers.

Third, the newspaper industry needs to re-examine how to protect and monetize its valuable print and online content.

Are online aggregators plagiarizing our work and profiting mightily by selling their ads around our content without giving us a cent? Or are they driving enough traffic and revenue to our Web sites that we justify the risk? While Google CEO Eric Schmidt was quoted recently as saying, "All information wants to be free," it's clear that the issue is not so simple—especially as Google continues to sell billions of dollars a year worth of advertising around original newspaper content.

Print ads may be poised to see a resurgence in value in the advertising community.

Finally, newspapers should improve the quality of their sales and marketing. While it's easy to blame what ails the newspaper industry on disruptive technologies, such as the Internet, newspaper companies need to revitalize their sales and marketing strategies and keep upgrading their personnel in these vital revenue-producing areas. Newspapers too often lag behind their competitors in understanding the ever-changing needs of their customers, whether they be advertisers, readers or nonreaders.

Many newspaper sales forces still are unwilling or unable to sell their value against competing media. For example, newspaper sales forces frequently struggle to extol the virtues of print advertising.

In fact, print ads may be poised to see a resurgence in value in the advertising community. They aren't skipped over by TiVos and DVRs, whose growing household penetration is destroying the television industry's revenue model. They don't scream at you for 20 minutes every hour like ad-saturated commercial radio. They don't cookie you, track your key-strokes and violate your privacy while selling your personal information as do many of the more manipulative Internet sites out there.

Plus, the Internet advertising world is suffering mightily from an overabundance of inventory and rapidly eroding CPMs (cost per thousand impressions—with *M* standing for the roman numeral for "thousand"), which are dropping like a rock toward zero. Remember, the return on investment and effectiveness of newspaper ads are well documented by extensive research. The value proposition is there, but it needs to be delivered to advertisers with impact and consistency.

In our rapidly changing society, newspapers, in print and online, can turn things around, reassert their relevance to readers and advertisers, and stage a comeback. It won't be easy or for the faint-hearted. It will take a lot of hard work. Not every new idea or strategy will succeed. But it can be done as long as we don't give up. We can't win this tough battle if we don't believe in our mission and in ourselves.

3

Newspapers Can Survive Through Consolidation

Jason Klein

Jason Klein is president and chief executive officer of Newspaper National Network, a sales and marketing partnership of twenty-five major newspaper companies.

The newspaper industry is up against a painful but necessary challenge: it must evolve. Most markets can no longer handle the sheer number of newspapers in existence. Consolidation will allow newspapers to exist alongside the blogosphere and other media options. Surviving newspapers should consider a single-price model for subscribers to read their news in print or digitally. Ultimately, these changes will benefit newspapers, readers, and advertisers.

The death knell for newspapers has been sounded too quickly. Newspapers are suffering from a confluence of factors, but many of their woes are self-imposed and have solutions, albeit painful ones. Newspapers have an enduring place in today's fragmented media world. The industry's survival depends on curing its structural ills and reshaping a new strategy for post-recession recovery.

Cutting Away the Deadwood

Like millions of American homeowners, many newspaper companies are buried in debt. It was piled on with the anticipation of never-ending profit growth and readily accepted by

Jason Klein, "Newspapers Down but Not Out," Newspaper National Network, April 22, 2009. Reprinted with permission.

bankers and optimistic buyers. Tribune Co., the Minneapolis *Star Tribune*, and the *Philadelphia Inquirer* and *Daily News* are already in Chapter 11 bankruptcy, and a number of other major companies will fall soon. They were not capitalized to survive a severe recession; Chapter 11 will provide them with a capital structure to see them through to a better economy.

The big U.S. air carriers have survived Chapter 11, and the big newspapers will too. Industry EBITDA (earnings before interest, tax, depreciation and amortization) margins are 14% to 16%, according to a recent J.P. Morgan analysis of public newspaper companies. While that's well below the peak of 25%, newspaper companies are generally still reasonably profitable.

The double whammy of excess debt and a severe recession exposes the broader structural issue of excess industry capacity: There are still too many newspapers in America. The newspaper industry will inevitably consolidate further. This is not a new phenomenon. When Horace Greeley published the *New York Tribune* in 1841, there were 12 papers in New York City jockeying for position. There were 1,773 daily newspapers in 1973, and at last count there are 1,422. The demise of afternoon papers accounts for the entire drop, as 886 of them have folded or shifted to the morning.

Many big markets, including San Francisco, Philadelphia, Minneapolis, Tampa and Dallas, are clearly over-newspapered.

Consolidation Not a Bad Thing

The core reality is that economics heavily favor one large newspaper per city—one reporting staff, one advertising sales staff, one management and long, efficient printing runs. The surviving lead paper will pick up circulation and advertisers and get a boost in financial viability.

This consolidation is not necessarily bad for readers or advertisers. While editorial variety in newspaper coverage will suffer, that is less important today with so many bloggers getting their views across. Advertisers will cheer large, unduplicated reach and simpler buying. Market forces will keep ad rates in check. Moreover, it is important to both readers and advertisers to see the medium on a sounder structural footing.

Consolidation will be painful, but it is inevitable. There are 500 markets in the U.S. While the largest markets can support several newspapers, most can't. Many big markets, including San Francisco, Philadelphia, Minneapolis, Tampa and Dallas, are clearly over-newspapered. If the average number of papers per market drops from two and a half to two, more than 250 newspapers would be absorbed by larger publishers.

The problem is partly government-induced. The [Richard] Nixon-era Newspaper Preservation Act of 1970 promoted the formation of Joint Operating Agreements [JOA] between competing papers. JOA markets such as Denver, Seattle and Detroit would be better served now by a single, large paper, and anti-trust enforcement should not stand in the way of that.

The newspaper industry that emerges from this recession will need all its strength to combat the single most pressing long-term threat to its business model: the conversion of readers to the web, and the impact of that on newspaper advertising, which is 80% of newspaper revenue.

Finding a Solution

The industry has pursued strategies to capitalize on the web for years. Hearst, Times Mirror and Knight Ridder were founding investors in Netscape, and CareerBuilder and Cars.com were founded by newspaper companies. They knew classified was doomed and tried to hedge their bets. Since then, newspapers have built their online audience to 75 million monthly unique visitors and are rivaled only by the portals in their local reach.

The problem is that nothing has generated enough revenue to offset the profit loss from the erosion of print advertising. The industry is coming to grips with the reality that online advertising, as it exists now, will never come close to replacing print advertising. The gospel of free online content is being questioned, and publishers are groping for new model.

They won't find it in viewing the web as a stand-alone business. The web will never support the kind of newsroom investment that's needed to cover local markets.

Newspaper print advertising is still massive—about $25 billion, even excluding classified.

Beyond Free Content

Newspaper publishers keep talking about the value of their content and the need to spread it across all distribution formats. Why not charge for it that way? One price, access across formats, print and digital. Readers pay for the content and can access it however they choose. Contrary to some impressions, newspapers' largest expense is people, not paper. A single price model would stem the decline of print subscriptions and increase the quality of the online audience.

That doesn't mean walking away from free online content. Some content would still be outside of the pay wall to attract news grazers, especially those outside of the home market.

Newspaper print advertising is still massive—about $25 billion, even excluding classified. One of the enduring truths of the business is that newspaper advertising drives retail sales and results. The problem is that price increases and circulation declines have advertisers questioning the cost and return on investment. A one-price model will help build back the value for advertisers.

The Next Round

If there is a bell tolling for newspapers, it's not a death knell; it's the beginning of a new round of their evolution. The forces of creative destruction will work to consolidate 1,422 daily newspapers into a more manageable number. And companies will dig themselves out from under their mountains of debt. Let the next round begin.

4

Newspapers No Longer Present a Viable Business Model

Henry Blodget

A former Wall Street analyst, Henry Blodget is chief executive officer and editor in chief of Business Insider.

Print advertising is what allows newspapers to pay for journalism. If content moves online, newspapers can no longer maintain a viable market share of advertising revenue. Calculating the strict financial challenges facing newspapers shows that they have no way to survive in the digital age.

It's easy to *say* that the *New York Times* [NYT] and other newspaper companies are screwed, but sometimes it helps to actually run the numbers. Do you know *why* they're screwed? It's actually not the cost of paper, ink, trucks, printing plants, and other physical distribution expenses. Rather, it's the cost of content creation.

Senior *New York Times* reporters believe they are underpaid, and, relative to other highly educated folks at the peak of their professions, they sure are. But relative to the *online* revenue they generate, those talented reporters, columnists, editors, and researchers actually cost a fortune.

Print Advertising Will Not Move Online

Newspaper content generates way more revenue in the physical world than it does online, because offline it can be packaged with classifieds and display ads and actually *sold*. In the

Henry Blodget, "Running the Numbers: Why Newspapers Are Screwed," *Business Insider*, April 10, 2007. Reprinted with permission.

online world, meanwhile, it has to be given away, and because classified ads are now run by classified sites and newspaper sites are only one of dozens of places where people get news, the advertising opportunity is comparatively tiny.

Let's pretend that, tomorrow morning, every print reader stops buying the paper, and instead, reads it online.

How tiny? Compete.com says the monthly reader base of NYTimes.com is about 7.5 million people. Offline circulation, meanwhile, is about 1.1 million. If we assume that the ratio of offline/online revenue at the Times Company is similar to that for the publication itself, the 7.5 million online readers generate 10% of the publication's revenue, and the 1.1 million offline sub[scriber]s generate 90%. Offline circ[ulation] and ad revenue are both declining. So let's think about what might happen as these trends continue.

Analyzing the Variables

Specifically, let's pretend that, tomorrow morning, every print reader stops buying the paper, and, instead, reads it online. To be safe, let's further assume that each offline "subscription" actually encompasses two or three readers. In other words, let's pretend that, tomorrow, print circulation goes to zero, and online readership jumps by 2.5 million. What would happen to the business?

- The company would eliminate paper, distribution, printing, and all other physical production costs.

- Online inventory (and, therefore, revenue) would increase by about 33% (7.5mm [million] to 10mm users)

- Content creation costs would *stay the same*. (The site would have to pay the freight for all the content it now gets for free).

- All print revenue—ads and circulation—would vaporize.

No, no, you say, the latter assumption is absurd. By the time print papers disappear, that $55 billion-plus of annual newspaper advertising will all have moved online, so the companies will be fine. Yes, the advertising will have moved online. But, no, newspapers won't be fine. Why not? Because only a small fraction of that $55 billion will flow to newspaper sites as opposed to eBay, Monster, Yahoo, Google, et al. We can quibble about the exact percentage, but just for kicks, let's pretend that, if the paper were suddenly eliminated, 25% of NYT's offline revenue would flow to NYTimes.com.

Running the Numbers

With these assumptions, we can make the following adjustments to the NYT's Q2 numbers. (Second Quarter earnings)

REVENUE:

- Cut offline revenue to zero

- Boost online revenue by 33% to account for increase in online readership

- Boost online revenue by 25% of offline revenue under assumption that some will follow online.

COSTS:

- Cut "raw materials" costs to zero.

- Cut "other" production costs to zero, under assumption that they are ALL print-production and distribution related (which they probably aren't)

- Reduce "wages and salaries" by 25%, under assumption that some are print-production and distribution related (which is probably too big a reduction)

- Reduce sales, general, and administrative costs by 33% to account for lower revenue base.

RESULTS:

Revenue drops by more than half, 40%–50% of employees get fired, and the company still loses money. Using the NYT's Q2 numbers and these assumptions, for example, revenue would have dropped from $789 million to $285 million. More importantly, EBITDA (earnings before interest, taxes, depreciation, and amortization) would have dropped from $118 million to $64 million. Which means that management would just be getting ready to fire a few hundred more people.

This, in short, is why newspapers are screwed.

5

A Nonprofit Model May Help Newspapers Survive

David Swensen and Michael Schmidt

David Swensen, the author of Pioneering Portfolio Management, *is the chief investment officer at Yale University, where Michael Schmidt is a financial analyst.*

Newspapers cannot survive using their current business model. Even the largest papers are struggling to stay afloat as content moves onto the Internet, where advertising cannot pay for the cost of news gathering. It is time for us to endow newspapers the way we endow colleges and universities. By giving newspapers nonprofit status and appealing to our nation's biggest philanthropists for funding, we can preserve the journalism necessary for a healthy democracy.

"The basis of our governments being the opinion of the people, the very first object should be to keep that right," Thomas Jefferson wrote in January 1787. "And were it left to me to decide whether we should have a government without newspapers or newspapers without a government, I should not hesitate to prefer the latter."

Today, we are dangerously close to having a government without newspapers. American newspapers shoulder the burden of considerable indebtedness with little cash on hand, as their profit margins have diminished or disappeared. Readers turn increasingly to the Internet for information—even though the Internet has the potential to be, in the words of the chief executive of Google, Eric Schmidt, "a cesspool" of false information. If Jefferson was right that a well-informed citizenry is the foundation of our democracy, then newspapers must be saved.

Although the problems that the newspaper industry faces are well known, no one has offered a satisfactory solution. But there is an option that might not only save newspapers but also make them stronger. Turn them into nonprofit, endowed institutions—like colleges and universities. Endowments would enhance newspapers' autonomy while shielding them from the economic forces that are now tearing them down.

In the standard business model, newspapers rely on revenues from circulation and advertising to pay for news coverage and generate healthy profits. In the past decade, however, as Americans embraced the Internet, newspaper circulation has declined every year. Advertising revenues, which are tied to circulation levels, fell even faster. Classified ads, in particular, suffered as the Web offered cheaper, easier and more effective alternatives.

Endowments would enhance newspapers' autonomy while shielding them from the economic forces that are now tearing them down.

America's pre-eminent papers exemplify the distress. Average profit margins at *The Washington Post* over the past five years have been about 25 percent less than what they had been in the previous 15 years. At *The New York Times*, the decline was more than 50 percent. The debt-laden Tribune Company, which operates *The Chicago Tribune, The Los Angeles Times* and six other daily papers, has filed for bankruptcy protection.

Newspapers nationwide, struggling to survive the economic turmoil, seek to refinance debt, issue equity and dispose of nonessential assets. These actions are short-term solutions to a systemic problem, Band-Aids for a gaping wound.

News organizations have cut costs, with grave consequences. Over the past three years, *The New York Times, The Wall Street Journal, The Washington Post, The Chicago Tribune, The Los Angeles Times* and *The San Francisco Chronicle* have trimmed their staffs. The number of American correspondents reporting from abroad fell by 25 percent from 2002 to 2006, and only a handful of American newspapers now operate foreign bureaus.

The advertising revenues that newspaper Web sites generate are not enough to sustain robust news coverage.

In a move that would have been unthinkable just last year, *The New York Times* recently began selling display advertising on its front page. Some papers have even shrunk physically, eliminating sections and decreasing paper size.

As long as newspapers remain for-profit enterprises, they will find no refuge from their financial problems. The advertising revenues that newspaper Web sites generate are not enough to sustain robust news coverage. Though *The New York Times* Web site attracted 20 million unique users in October, Web-driven revenues support only an estimated 20 percent of the paper's current staff.

As newspapers go digital, their business model erodes. A 2008 research report from Sanford C. Bernstein & Company explained, "The notion that the enormous cost of real newsgathering might be supported by the ad load of display advertising down the side of the page, or by the revenue share from having a Google search box in the corner of the page, or even by a 15-second teaser from Geico prior to a news clip, is idiotic on its face."

By endowing our most valued sources of news we would free them from the strictures of an obsolete business model and offer them a permanent place in society, like that of America's colleges and universities. Endowments would transform newspapers into unshakable fixtures of American life, with greater stability and enhanced independence that would allow them to serve the public good more effectively.

An endowment would promote journalistic independence.

As educational and literary organizations devoted to the "promotion of social welfare," endowed newspapers would benefit from Section 501(c)(3) of the I.R.S. code, which provides exemption from taxes on income and allows tax deductions for people who make contributions to eligible organizations.

One constraint on an endowed institution is the prohibition in the same law against trying to "influence legislation" or "participate in any campaign activity for or against political candidates." While endowed newspapers would need to refrain from endorsing candidates for public office, they would still be free to participate forcefully in the debate over issues of public importance. The loss of endorsements seems minor in the context of the opinion-heavy Web.

Aside from providing stability, an endowment would promote journalistic independence. The best-run news organizations insulate reporters from pressures to produce profits or to placate advertisers. But endowed news organizations would be in an ideal situation—with no pressure from stockholders or advertisers at all.

How large an endowment would a newspaper need? The news-gathering operations at *The New York Times* cost a little more than $200 million a year. Assuming some additional outlay for overhead, it would require an endowment of approximately $5 billion (assuming a 5 percent annual payout rate). Newspapers with smaller newsrooms would require smaller endowments.

Note that just as endowed educational institutions charge tuition, endowed newspapers would generate incremental revenues from hard-copy sales and online subscriptions. If revenues were to exceed the costs of distribution, the endowment requirement would decline.

Many newspapers will not weather the digital storm on their own. Only a handful of foundations and wealthy individuals have the money required to endow, and thereby preserve, our nation's premier news-gathering organizations. Enlightened philanthropists must act now or watch a vital component of American democracy fade into irrelevance.

6

Newspapers Should Consider a Hybrid Nonprofit/For-Profit Model

James T. Hamilton

James T. Hamilton directs the DeWitt Wallace Center for Media and Democracy at Duke University's Sanford School of Public Policy in Durham, North Carolina.

The continued downsizing of newspaper employees is a sober re-minder of the challenges facing the traditional media industry. We must find a way to let journalism continue to perform its important watchdog role in our society. Encouraging newspapers to transition to nonprofit status is one possible solution. Another is allowing newspapers to operate as low-profit limited liability corporations. Although there are issues to consider, this hybrid approach could offer the right amount of flexibility for both journalists and investors.

Since the start of 2008, 26,000 jobs have been eliminated at metro newspapers in the U.S. [as of August 17, 2009.] Papers in Denver, Seattle and elsewhere have ceased operations.

What this means for you, the reader, is that millions of stories won't be written this year. So as state and local officials struggle to make tough budget choices, for instance, there are fewer full-time journalists working the government beat and ferreting out questionable proposals for spending your public tax dollars.

James T. Hamilton, "Nonprofit Model Makes Sense for Newspapers," *The Atlanta Journal-Constitution*, August 17 2009. Reprinted with permission.

Journalists Have Been Our Watchdogs

Over the years, journalists at daily newspapers have held our officials accountable by going to meetings, poring through documents and developing sources. The resulting tales of corruption, waste and abuse of power have influenced the course of public policy and affected which politicians held office.

Papers are struggling today because, among other reasons, they have lost a good chunk of their advertising revenue to the Internet. At a time of dwindling revenue, many newspapers simply do not have a profit incentive to engage in significant watchdog or accountability journalism.

A Nonprofit Approach

One possible solution to rescuing the watchdog function of the press is to allow newspapers to operate as nonprofits. If a newspaper were run as a nonprofit, this would allow people who valued the impact of its stories to donate and receive a tax deduction.

The list of media outlets that have nonprofit tax status is growing and includes magazines such as *Harper's*, *Mother Jones*, and *The American Spectator* and newly formed Web outlets that cover local news. As some newspapers try to emerge from or avoid bankruptcy, the option of running as a nonprofit would provide an additional revenue stream to support reporting.

One possible solution to rescuing the watchdog function of the press is to allow newspapers to operate as nonprofits.

Media and nonprofit leaders who recently met at Duke [University] identified several steps the federal government could take to make it easier for struggling daily newspapers to transition to nonprofits. For example, the Internal Revenue

Service [IRS] currently has the power to issue tax guidelines that would make clear that metro daily newspapers could be run as nonprofits.

A Low-Profit Approach

Additionally, Congress could speed the development of new forms of media organization, such as the low-profit limited liability (L3C) corporation. L3Cs are companies with low profits but high positive spillovers on their communities.

A newspaper run as an L3C could draw many different types of investors. Foundations interested in accountability coverage could make a program-related investment in the L3C and state up front they did not expect a high rate of return. Socially conscious investors who care about local news could also invest in the L3C and accept only a modest rate of return. With these two sets of investors accepting lower rates, a third set of investors in search of a market rate of return also could be willing to invest in a newspaper.

Newspapers have always been skittish about taking money from certain sources. They obviously don't want to have the appearance of a conflict of interest in their coverage.

If a metro newspaper were run as an L3C, the presence of investors who focused on the quality of public affairs coverage would help managers make the case for watchdog stories. And if the L3C ended up doing well and doing good at the same time, the taxes on any profits would be paid as they were distributed among the investors.

To date, no newspaper has transformed into a L3C, in part because of uncertainties over how foundation investments in them might be treated.

Last year [2008], Congress considered legislation that would have required the IRS to rule quickly on foundation requests for approval of program-related investments. The legislation also would have made clear that foundation investments in L3Cs were appropriate. If Congress passed the appropriate legislation, this could hasten experimentation with these new forms of media hybrids.

Funding Sources

Newspapers have always been skittish about taking money from certain sources. They obviously don't want to have the appearance of a conflict of interest in their coverage, especially if the reporting was about an investor. Similarly, asking the government to fund coverage of government would be very risky.

But having the government make it easier for newspapers to run as nonprofits would allow those who valued journalism to support it more easily. If the IRS and Congress pave the road for media hybrids, it will then be up to readers and foundations to provide the resources to power these nonprofit watchdogs.

7

Journalism Is Being Undermined by Blogs

Michael Skube

Michael Skube is a Pulitzer Prize–winning author and associate professor at Elon University's School of Communications in North Carolina.

Instead of raising the level of public debate, bloggers are diluting it. By insisting on the privileges of journalistic protection for what is essentially a hobby, bloggers challenge the preeminence of quality reporting. Journalists like Claude Sitton remind us of the persistence and risk taking that are necessary to tell the stories that make a real difference.

The late Christopher Lasch once wrote that public affairs generally and journalism in particular suffered not from too little information but from entirely too much. What was needed, he argued, was robust debate. Lasch, a historian by training but a cultural critic by inclination, was writing in 1990, when the Internet was not yet a part of everyday life and bloggers did not exist.

Bloggers now are everywhere among us, and no one asks if we don't need more full-throated advocacy on the Internet. The blogosphere is the loudest corner of the Internet, noisy with disputation, manifesto-like postings and an unbecoming hatred of enemies real and imagined.

And to think most bloggers are doing all this on the side. "No man but a blockhead," the stubbornly sensible

Michael Skube, "Blogs: All the Noise That Fits," *Los Angeles Times*, August 19, 2007. Reprinted with permission.

[eighteenth-century author] Samuel Johnson said, "ever wrote but for money." Yet here are people, whole brigades of them, happy to write for free. And not just write. Many of the most active bloggers—Andrew Sullivan, Matthew Yglesias, Joshua Micah Marshall and the contributors to the *Huffington Post*—are insistent partisans in political debate. Some reject the label "journalist," associating it with what they contemptuously call MSM (mainstream media); just as many, if not more, consider themselves a new kind of "citizen journalist" dedicated to broader democratization.

The Rise of Bloggers

Markos Moulitsas Zuniga, whose popular blog Daily Kos has been a force among antiwar activists, cautioned bloggers last week [August 2007] "to avoid the right-wing acronym MSM." It implied, after all, that bloggers were on the fringe. To the contrary, he wrote, "we are representatives of the mainstream, and the country is embracing what we're selling."

In 2004, bloggers were awarded press credentials to the Democratic National Convention.

Moulitsas foresees bloggers becoming the watchdogs that watch the watchdog: "We need to keep the media honest, but as an institution, it's important that they exist and do their job well." The tone is telling: breezy, confident, self-congratulatory. Subtly, it implies bloggers have all the liberties of a traditional journalist but few of the obligations.

There is at least some reason for activists like Moulitsas to see themselves as the new wave. Last year, [2006] the California 6th District Court of Appeal gave bloggers the legal victory they wanted when it ruled that they were protected under the state's reporter shield law. Other, more symbolic victories have come their way too. In 2004, bloggers were awarded press credentials to the Democratic National Convention. And earlier this month in Chicago, at a convention sponsored by Daily Kos, a procession of Democratic presidential hopefuls offered full salutes, knowing that bloggers are busy little bees in organizing political support and fundraising.

And yet none of this makes them journalists, even in the sense Lasch seemed to be advocating.

Lowering the Quality of Public Debate

"What democracy requires," Lasch wrote in "The Lost Art of Argument," "is vigorous public debate, not information. Of course, it needs information too, but the kind of information it needs can only be generated by debate. We do not know what we need until we ask the right questions, and we can identify the right questions only by subjecting our own ideas about the world to the test of public controversy."

If there's anything bloggers want more than an audience, it's knowing they are making a difference in politics.

There was something appealing about this argument—one that no blogger would reject—when Lasch advanced it almost two decades ago. But now we have the opportunity to witness it in practice, thanks to the blogosphere, and the results are less than satisfying. One gets the uneasy sense that the blogosphere is a potpourri of opinion and little more. The opinions are occasionally informed, often tiresomely cranky and never in doubt. Skepticism, restraint, a willingness to suspend judgment and to put oneself in the background—these would not seem to be a blogger's trademarks.

Nuance Not Necessary for Blogging

But they are, more often than not, trademarks of the kind of journalism that makes a difference. And if there is anything bloggers want more than an audience, it's knowing they are making a difference in politics. They are, to give them their due, changing what is euphemistically called the national "conversation." But what is the nature of that change? Does it deepen our understanding? Does it broaden our perspective?

It's hard to answer yes to such questions, if only because they presuppose a curiosity and inquiry for which raw opinion is ill-suited. Sometimes argument—a word that elevates blogosphere comment to a level it seldom attains on its own—gains from old-fashioned gumshoe reporting. Compelling examples abound. On the same day I read of the Daily Kos convention in Chicago, I finished "The Race Beat: The Press, the Civil Rights Struggle and the Awakening of a Nation," winner this year [2007] of the Pulitzer Prize for history. No one looms larger in the book by Gene Roberts Jr. and Hank Klibanoff than Claude Sitton, whose reporting in the *New York Times* in the 1960s would become legendary.

Epitomizing the Journalistic Spirit

Full disclosure: I once worked for Sitton at the *News & Observer* in Raleigh, N.C., after he had left the *Times*, and I knew that he and others, including Karl Fleming, had put themselves in harm's way simply to report a story. I naively asked Sitton once if he had encountered veiled threats. "Veiled?" he asked. "They were more than veiled."

He recounted the time in Philadelphia, Miss., when "a few rednecks—drunk, shotguns in the back of their truck—showed up at the Holiday Inn where Fleming and I were staying." The locals invited the big-city reporters—Sitton from the *Times*, Fleming from *Newsweek*—to come out and see the farm. "I told 'em, 'Look, you shoot us and there'll be a dozen more just like us in the morning. You going to shoot them too?'"

When I knew him, Sitton seldom mentioned those dangers of 20 years earlier. What mattered was the story, and the people swept up in it. But it was his vivid, detailed reporting that, as Roberts and Klibanoff write, caught the attention of the Kennedy White House and brought the federal government to intervene in a still-segregated South.

The more important a story, the more incidental our opinions become.

Reporting Should Supersede Opinion

In our time, the *Washington Post*'s reporting, in late 2005, of the CIA's secret overseas prisons and its painstaking reports this year on problems at Walter Reed Army Medical Center— both of which won Pulitzer Prizes—were not exercises in armchair commentary. The disgrace at Walter Reed, true enough, was first mentioned in a blog, but the full scope of that story could not have been undertaken by a blogger or, for that matter, an Op-Ed columnist, whose interest is in expressing an opinion quickly and pungently. Such a story demanded time, thorough fact-checking and verification and, most of all, perseverance. It's not something one does as a hobby.

The more important the story, the more incidental our opinions become. Something larger is needed: the patient sifting of fact, the acknowledgment that assertion is not evidence and, as the best writers understand, the depiction of real life. Reasoned argument, as well as top-of-the-head comment on the blogosphere, will follow soon enough, and it should. But what lodges in the memory, and sometimes knifes us in the heart, is the fidelity with which a writer observes and tells. The word has lost its luster, but we once called that reporting.

8

Quality Journalism Is Essential Regardless of the Medium

Jill Abramson

Jill Abramson is the managing editor for news at The New York Times.

The proliferation of digital information and economic cuts to investigative journalism have led to a lowering of quality news content. Quality journalism requires money and time, but we can be optimistic about the future of journalism because it speaks to a basic human need. Quality journalism does not require paper and can coexist with other types of information and commentary. The Internet has the capacity to increase journalistic quality in some cases, but we must experiment with new business solutions that protect journalists. Not all news companies will survive, and those that do will do so through a variety of strategies.

It is well past time to reject the artificial divide between the guardians of print journalism and the boosters of blogs, Internet news aggregators, and other new media. Rather than battling over whether bloggers are real journalists or whether newspapers need to be preserved, the fight should focus more on championing serious, quality journalism, no matter who produces it or where it is published.

Rigorous news-gathering plays a vital role in our society, especially in holding the largest and most important institutions accountable. It is easy to forget how afraid of centralized power the founders of this country were, and how the press was envisioned by them as a bulwark protecting the free flow of critical information about the powerful. No single form of news-gathering, single platform, or single news organization can by itself uphold this mission or supply all the intelligence, energy, and muscle needed to dig behind the most complex stories and cover them with the kind of depth that has elevated journalism's civic role over the last century.

There is a human need and desire for quality journalism. In the Age of Too Much Information, it seems absurd to argue that the supply of quality news is running low, but it is. The most expensive forms of news-gathering, especially international coverage and investigative reporting, are suffering deep cuts in many of the country's newsrooms—which are themselves dwindling in number. While many promising, Internet-based news sites have sprung up over the past few years to help fill the gap, they have not kept pace with what has been lost.

Meanwhile, during a difficult digital transition, the business model for supplying quality journalism has come under severe stress, and an industry-wide rethinking is under way. Until now, the idea that news on the Web should be free has prevailed, and during years of expansive advertising, this ethos saw the flowering of thousands of different news sites and a healthy democratization of voices of authority. Journalism became more participatory and collaborative. "Content, like wild horses, wanted to be free," wrote Richard Perez-Peña in *The New York Times* in December 2009, and consumers grew accustomed to a huge assortment of free news, photos, and videos.

But the severe economic downturn, accompanied by steep advertising cutbacks, has meant that new revenue sources are needed to sustain quality journalism. It takes millions of dollars annually, to cite but one example, for the *Times* and the few other news organizations able and willing to commit the necessary resources to maintain fully staffed bureaus in Baghdad and Kabul for coverage of two international wars. Most major news organizations are now weighing whether to ask their online readers to pay for at least some of their content, as some newspapers already have. The *Times* recently announced it would institute a paid metered model on its website and some other digital platforms in 2011.

In the Age of Too Much Information, it seems absurd to argue that the supply of quality news is running low, but it is.

Many different versions of pay walls have been proposed, as well as partnerships among the major news-gatherers. While this may limit consumer choice and reduce the audiences for some paid sites, media companies that once assumed that advertising on the Web would continue to expand exponentially are faced with the cold reality that without shifting some of the cost burden to consumers, they may be forced into ever more drastic cuts or even face the prospect of shutting down. These challenges have been especially acute for the newspaper business.

Indeed, just as newspaper executives were trying to hang on and adapt to new realities, the economic crisis of late 2008 hit. For newspapers, disappointing third quarters were followed by murderous fourth quarters, with huge drops in advertising revenue as many sectors—especially help wanted, financial, and real estate—severely cut their ad budgets.

Alex S. Jones, a Pulitzer Prize–winning journalist, provides a cogent history of these stormy times in his recently published book, *Losing the News*. He notes the constant drumbeat of bad news, including the shuttering of foreign and domestic news bureaus. As testament to the rough times, he cites his own inbox crammed with email messages from newspaper journalists who have lost their jobs. In a particularly chilling example, Jones describes the excellent reporting done by *The San Diego Union-Tribune*, which won a Pulitzer for its investigation into allegations of corruption surrounding former California Representative Randal "Duke" Cunningham. The paper's Washington bureau, which did most of the reporting on that story, was closed during a round of cost-cutting along with the Washington bureaus of many other newspapers.

Given that the news media were criticized for being too compliant during the Bush administration, it would seem a dangerous and inopportune moment to be cutting the collective investigative muscle of journalism in the nation's capital. Indeed, without robust investigative reporting by *The Washington Post* on secret CIA prisons or *The New York Times'* revelations about warrantless eavesdropping by the NSA, readers might still be ignorant about such secret counterterrorism policies. Given the keen national interest in the Obama administration and in the administration's approach to governing, news organizations should be beefing up, not diminishing their coverage. Without aggressive, professional reporting, the public might not have known about the special deals buried within the health care reform legislation or how Wall Street is currently lobbying to water down new financial regulations.

The few cities that still had competing newspapers have seen the weaker ones rail: for example, the closing of the print editions of the *Seattle Post-Intelligencer* and the *Rocky Mountain News*. Two major metropolitan newspapers, the *San Francisco Chronicle* and the *Minneapolis Star-Tribune*, have been teetering on the brink and have endured extremely deep staff cuts. Other storied names, like the Tribune Company and Knight-Ridder, have filed for bankruptcy or gone out of business.

International reporting has also taken a terrible hit. In 2003, there were more than a thousand foreign journalists covering the war in Iraq. Today that number has dwindled to fewer than one hundred. Even in major and news-intense cities like Moscow, there are few U.S. journalists left, with the recent retreats of *The Baltimore Sun, Chicago Tribune*, and *The Philadelphia Inquirer. The Boston Globe*, a member of the *Times* family and a newspaper with a distinguished tradition of international reporting was forced to close all of its foreign bureaus and eliminate the job of foreign editor. The *Times'* bureau chief in Cairo, Michael Slackman, said that when he was assigned there less than five years ago he had an array of print and broadcast competitors. Now he has just a single full-time American newspaper competitor: the *Los Angeles Times.* Full-time American correspondents are seldom seen in many other international capitals.

Given the keen national interest in the Obama administration and in the administration's approach to governing, news organizations should be beefing up, not diminishing, their coverage.

Large layoffs in newsrooms have become a daily reality. It was sobering to read the recent assessment offered by one of journalism's cheerleaders, Warren Buffett, who in his 2007 report to shareholders wrote: "When an industry's underlying economics are crumbling, talented management may slow the rate of decline. Eventually, though, eroding fundamentals will overwhelm managerial brilliance." Buffett took little comfort in the Internet as a remedy for the decline, noting, "The economic potential of a newspaper Internet site—given the many alternative sources of information and entertainment that are free and only a click away—is at best a small fraction of that existing in the past for a print newspaper facing no competition." Although Buffett reiterated his belief in the centrality of a free and vigorous press, even he conceded that if the news became an irreversible cash drain on his company, he might be forced to sell his beloved *Buffalo News.*

At *The New York Times* there is a fierce determination to protect the core of our news-gathering, including the most robust international and investigative coverage. As part of a business strategy developed years ago, we have integrated our Web and print operations, overcoming a once ingrained internal culture that sprouted from the world of print. We have avoided some of the destructive rivalries between different platforms that have erupted at other news organizations. While the Web has added to the workload of many in our newsroom, it has also excited and broadened our staff, who have learned to tell stories in new ways. For our journalists based abroad, the Web has given an immediacy and greater impact to their work that goes beyond the satisfaction of seeing their articles in print.

For example, when the *Times* published a recent investigative series on Putin's Russia, the articles were translated into Russian simultaneously so that readers there could dissect the stories and post their comments, which were translated back into English on the *Times'* site. So the Web does, quite literally, democratize the news.

Quality journalism is produced on many platforms. I applaud the announcement that *The Huffington Post* will be underwriting original investigative reporting, perhaps giving work to journalists who have lost their jobs. ProPublica, a nonprofit established to produce the highest quality investigative journalism, is also doing important work. (I am a member of ProPublica's outside Board of Advisors.) In the international arena, GlobalPost is supplying quality content by professional journalists, some of whom were laid off from traditional news companies, and is partnering with several of these same news organizations, including CBS News.

However, when millions of voices boom on the Web, there is also space for rumor, incorrect facts, and just plain nonsense. Amateur citizen-journalists sometimes do not have the skills and background to produce the most accurate journalism. Newspapers, with professional reporters and editors, still account for breaking the vast majority of important news stories, and some websites and bloggers are mainly drawing from news already published by newspapers. On some stories, especially those dealing with intelligence matters or complex business deals, it can take months for experienced reporters to convince sources to talk and for the reporters to obtain sensitive documents. They win the confidence of their sources because of their knowledge, the depth of their reporting, their courage, and their reputation. The work of *Times* correspondent and author Dexter Filkin in Iraq and Afghanistan, for example, required years of training and experience.

For our journalists based abroad, the Web has given an immediacy and greater impact to their work that goes beyond the satisfaction of seeing their articles in print.

Our challenge, then, is to find a business model that suits Web-based journalism while sustaining quality journalism. Advertising on the Web, even in more robust times, is still less profitable than advertising in print. Readers spend less time with the *Times* online than in print: on average, a visitor to the website spends about thirty-six minutes per month, just a little more than the typical print *Times* reader would spend per day. As a 2007 report by Harvard's Joan Shorenstein Center on the Press, Politics and Public Policy notes, "It is estimated that a newspaper has to attract two or three dozen online readers to make up for, in terms of lost advertising revenue, the defection of a single hard-copy reader."

While some media analysts have argued that newspapers should ditch their expensive printing presses and elaborate distribution chains and go Web-only, it is hard to envision, especially in the current economy, how enough revenue would be generated to support a paper's large and highly experienced news-gathering staff.

Everywhere, the self-assured prophets of journalism are spouting their proclamations: readers will never pay for news on the Web; readers must pay for news on the Web. Journalism must find a way to generate more profits; journalism must become a nonprofit.

Anyone who claims to have a silver-bullet solution isn't playing straight. There isn't one answer that will save every news organization. The differences within the news industry, from small, hyperlocal newspapers and websites to national publications like *The Wall Street Journal* and *The New York Times*, are too vast. Not every newspaper is going to make the transition across the digital divide.

There have been some serious proposals put forth that bear consideration, but almost all carry risks. As *The Economist* noted in August 2009:

> It will not be easy. For ten years readers have been enjoying free news online, and the BBC, public-radio stations and commercial television news outlets like CNN will continue to supply it. A newspaper that tries to charge will jeopardize online advertising, which often accounts for 10–15% of revenues.

One approach is to erect a pay wall around stories on the Web, while making an exception for print subscribers. With its business news focus, *The Wall Street Journal* has charged for online subscriptions for years, but its formula may not necessarily apply to other general-interest newspapers. Some publications have charged for a digital simulacrum of their print editions, which certain readers find easier to navigate than a newspaper website. (*The New York Times* offers the Times Reader.) The *Financial Times* keeps readers on a meter, charging those who look at more than a certain number of stories a month. Some, including former *Time* magazine editor Walter Isaacson, have proposed micropayments for individual articles or a menu of coverage. Smartphones, with customized news applications, are another possible source of paid revenue.

The best minds in journalism are mapping out new strategies to adjust their business models for producing quality journalism in the digital age. I am confident that in the next few years we will see experimentation and adjustments along the way.

Not every newspaper is going to make the transition across the digital divide.

Decades from now, the quality newspapers that remain may not be literally on paper. They may be on portable tablets or some other device we haven't yet envisioned. But journalism will continue to thrive. My optimism is based on the fact that there is a human craving for trustworthy information about the world we live in—information that is tested, investigated, sorted, checked again, analyzed, and presented in a cogent form.

Yet people don't crave just information. They seek judgment from someone they can trust, who can ferret out information, dig behind it, and make sense of it. They want analytic depth, skepticism, context, and a presentation that honors their intelligence. They want stories that are elegantly told and compelling, with quality pictures and videos. And they want to be part of the conversation.

In print, the *Times* has developed a loyal audience of highly educated and informed readers who are passionate about their relationship with the newspaper and who have proved willing to pay handsomely for it. While Web news browsing and the habits of Internet readers are different, the digital audience also turns to trusted brands and reliable news filters. During the months leading to the 2008 election, for example, ny times.com had an audience of more than 20 million unique visitors per month. These readers, of course, were also likely supplementing their journalism diet with other sources of political news. The process of creating an engaged and informed citizenry takes a variety of forms, none necessarily more perfect than the other.

Quality journalism plays an irreplaceable role in our society. It is time to move past all the shouting over which platform or which business model is best and to join in an urgent and collective effort to protect what matters most: quality journalism and the journalists who create it.

9

New Media Require New Ways to Evaluate Information

Olivia Scheck

Olivia Scheck is a student at Yale University and a guest columnist for www.3quarksdaily.com.

We are living through a difficult time, when the collective noise of the Internet both increases the amount of information we receive and decreases its quality. We have access to a tremendous volume of ideas and opinions, but the aggregate is not quite enough to replace the journalism we are losing. While there is reason to be optimistic about the future, we must adopt a new way of taking in information that is aligned with our having greater individual responsibility to decide what is valuable.

I am embarrassed to say that before this weekend I had never visited Edge.org.

I was first directed to the site [in March 2010] by a post on 3QD [3 Quarks Daily], and I have remained there ever since, devouring responses to the 2010 Edge Annual Question, "How is the internet changing the way you think?"

There are many wonderful ideas to glean from this incredible collection of essays, but I was especially interested in what the replies suggested for the future of journalism and—perhaps a separate issue—the future of journalists.

More Perspectives, More Value?

In an article on Edge that is not actually part of the 2010 Question, the financial journalist Charles Leadbeater uses the

Olivia Scheck, "What the Internet Will Mean for Journalism and Journalists: Insights from the Edge," www.3quarksdaily.com, March 15, 2010. Reprinted with permission.

example of open source software to suggest what the internet may allow in other cultural realms.

"The more people that test out a programme the quicker the bugs will be found," Leadbeater explains. "The more people that see a collection of content, from more vantage points, the more likely they are to find value in it, probably value that a small team of professional curators may have missed."

The application of this analogy to journalism is obvious and, to varying degrees, the concept has already been put into practice. The blog/traditional news hybrid site, Talking Points Memo [TPM], for instance, invites readers to contribute leads and even comb through government documents on their behalf. *TPM's* crowd-sourcing strategy has allowed the website's comparatively tiny staff of reporters to break several major stories, including the U.S. Attorney firing scandal. There is also *The Huffington Post*, which famously employs unpaid "citizen journalists" and "volunteer bloggers," in addition to paid editorial staff.

Threatening Quality Journalism

More generally, the surge in claims and opinions that now appear on the internet would seem, by sheer probability, to have increased the amount of accurate or useful information that is available to the public. Of course, for every instance like the TPM U.S. Attorney story, in which the work of amateur internet journalists has had beneficial consequences for society, there have been, one assumes, many more instances of misinformation, slander and inanity. There is also the problematic tendency of independent online publishers to redistribute professional content without compensating authors.

As Leadbeater notes, many believe that the explosion of amateur-created content, combined with the increased ease of copying professionally-made content will ". . . undermine the creation of high quality commercial cultural products," by making it financially unprofitable. Additionally, Leadbeater writes, "They worry we are heading for a culture of constant interference, noise and distraction, in which the more music and writing, photos and films there are, the more cultural chaos and social disorder there will be."

In other words, critics argue that the internet threatens quality cultural content, including quality journalism, in two ways: (1) by undermining the business models that currently finance it, and (2) by obscuring it in noise and distraction.

Avoiding Another Dark Age

Clay Shirky, author and professor of interactive telecommunications at NYU, offers a terrific analysis of the first issue, in his response to the 2010 Edge Question:

> This shock of inclusion, where professional media gives way to participation by two billion amateurs (a threshold we will cross this year) means that average quality of public thought has collapsed; when anyone can say anything any time, how could it not? If all that happens from this influx of amateurs is the destruction of existing models for producing high-quality material, we would be at the beginning of another Dark Ages. So it falls to us to make sure that isn't all that happens.

While Shirky acknowledges the dangers of a world in which the forces of the internet have diminished the financial incentive to produce quality cultural content, he calls, optimistically, for the creation of alternative models or alternative types of content.

But even if some set of alternatives is developed to continue the production of quality material, it is not clear that such content would be produced by professionals or for commercial organizations.

A Glimpse of the Future

TPM and *The Huffington Post* are two examples of what this change might look like for journalism. Programs like Ushahidi, a web platform that allows users to aggregate information on maps and timelines via text message, might also help fill the vacancy left by old media.

I share Shirky's optimism that the internet will find ways to replace the systems that it destroys, but I also share his belief that this period of transition will be a tough one.

"It is our misfortune to live through the largest increase in expressive capability in the history of the human race," he writes, half-ironically, "a misfortune because surplus always breaks more things than scarcity. Scarcity means valuable things become more valuable, a conceptually easy change to integrate. Surplus, on the other hand, means previously valuable things stop being valuable, which freaks people out."

The second threat that the internet poses to quality cultural content—the threat of drowning it in noise—is also addressed by several Edge contributors.

The surge in content created by the internet both detracts from and enhances our consumption of cultural material, including news.

Survival of the Fittest

German intellectual, Frank Schirrmacher, for instance, proposes a conception of the internet as a Darwinian environment in which ideas compete for survival and the limited resource is attention.

"We have a population explosion of ideas, but not enough brains to cover them," Schirrmacher explains.

As ideas battle for survival, we become the arbiters of which ideas live and which ideas die. But weeding through them is cognitively demanding, and our minds may be ill-suited to the task.

Conversely, in his response to the 2010 Question, the former Executive Editor of *Wired*, Kevin Kelly, suggests that when it comes to journalism, the act of weeding may actually confer a more nuanced appreciation of the issues of the day:

> For every accepted piece of knowledge I find, there is within easy reach someone who challenges the fact. Every fact has its anti-fact ... I am less interested in Truth, with a capital T, and more interested in truths, plural. I feel the subjective has an important role in assembling the objective from many data points.

As ideas battle for survival, we become the arbiters of which ideas live and which ideas die.

It seems to me that Schirrmacher and Kelly are both correct. The surge in content created by the internet both detracts from and enhances our consumption of cultural material, including news. The net effect, of course, remains to be seen. What is clear is that we must alter our approach to absorbing information.

Changing the Relationship

The science historian, George Dyson, may have put it best in his reply to the 2010 Question, which analogized the experience of modern web surfers to that of indigenous boat builders in the North Pacific Ocean.

"In the North Pacific Ocean," Dyson explains, "there were two approaches to boatbuilding"—the approach used by the Aleuts, who pieced their boats together using fragments of beach-combed wood, and the approach used by the Tlingit, who carved each vessel out of a single dugout tree.

The two methods yielded similar results, Dyson tells us, each group employing the minimum allotment of available resources. However, they did so by opposite means.

"The flood of information unleashed by the Internet has produced a similar cultural split," Dyson argues. "We used to be kayak builders, collecting all available fragments of information to assemble the framework that kept us afloat. Now, we have to learn to become dugout-canoe builders, discarding unnecessary information to reveal the shape of knowledge hidden within."

10

Newspapers Are Thriving in Developing Countries

The Economist

The Economist *is a weekly publication that covers world affairs.*

Newspapers are doing well in developing and even middle-income countries. Relative prosperity along with literacy campaigns increase demand for print media. Some countries enjoy more press freedoms than others, but newspapers seem to be proliferating regardless of these standards. There are opportunities for investment and advertising.

It may not be much consolation to the hard-pressed hacks of the rich world, but in many developing countries the newspaper business is booming. According to figures released in June [2008] by the World Association of Newspapers (WAN), an industry body based in Paris, newspapers in Brazil increased by some 12% last year [2007]. Over the past five years [2003–2008], circulation has gone up by more than 22%. In India, sales rose by 11%, bringing the five-year increase to more than 35%. Pakistan's newspaper market grew by almost as much in the same period. The trend is similar elsewhere in Asia and Latin America.

Newspapers as Status Symbols

The demand for news tends to go up as people enter the workforce, earn more money, invest it and so begin to feel that they have more of a stake in their society. Literacy rates also rise in tandem with wealth. For the newly literate, flipping through a newspaper in public is a potent and satisfying symbol of achievement.

Literacy campaigns by the government and NGOs [nongovernmental organizations] account for much of the increase in sales of Indian newspapers, according to Ashok Dasgupta of the *Hindu*, a big Indian daily based in Chennai. Hiring is brisk, he says, and new papers and magazines are "cropping up every day". Most are small, but the number of big, high-quality national business dailies has risen from four in 2006 to six today [2008]. A seventh will appear later this year.

China's vast oversight apparatus keeps tabs on big and small outlets alike. But newspapers are thriving there, too.

Press: Free and Not So Free

Publishers in India benefit from a long tradition of press freedom. But papers in countries with more meddling governments are also, by and large, doing well. This is especially true of small newspapers. Governments with limited resources are often ill-equipped to monitor a profusion of local and regional newspapers. In Mali, for example, newspapers are popping up "like mushrooms", says Souleymane Kanté, the local manager for World Education, an American NGO that aims to eradicate illiteracy. The Malian government keeps large national publications in line, Mr Kanté says, but local and regional papers have some breathing room.

China's vast oversight apparatus keeps tabs on big and small outlets alike. But newspapers are thriving there, too. In the past five years sales have increased by more than 20% to 107m [million] copies a day. (By comparison, daily sales in America amount to some 50m.) China's growing wealth helps to explain this. So does a high level of literacy, thanks in part to the Communist Party's investment in education.

Shaun Rein, of the China Market Research Group in Shanghai, says there are also other factors at work. Because all Chinese newspapers are state-owned, they will probably remain cheap even as costs increase and advertisers move online. And Beijing's struggle to limit corruption may also play a part. Some officials see local publications as allies in the effort to unmask crooked regional and municipal authorities, and so favour lengthening reporters' leashes. Others seem to disapprove, leading to rumours of a debate within the upper echelons of the party—unreported by Chinese media, of course.

Newspapers are doing well in middle-income countries, too, according to WAN. In Argentina, for example, newspaper circulation jumped more than 7% last year. Manuel Mora y Araujo, of IPSOS, a consultancy, says media groups from America and other rich countries have not been investing in Argentine news organisations, possibly because their own problems mean that they cannot afford to. Nonetheless, he says, "The press isn't worried—there's tons of advertising."

11

Ethnic Newspapers Serve a Critical Role in Communities

Sally Lehrman

Sally Lehrman is the Knight-Ridder/San Jose Mercury News Chair in Journalism and the Public Interest at Santa Clara University in California.

Ethnic newspapers fill a larger role in American journalism than their tiny—and now diminishing—staffs might suggest. On issues such as race relations and immigration, ethnic media offer information and alternative perspectives that are not often covered by the predominately white journalists and sources of mainstream news.

AsianWeek, San Francisco's English-language weekly for Asian Americans, and *San Francisco Bay View*, which has served the black community there for three decades, both have dumped their print editions. *Siglo21*, a Spanish-language paper published in Lawrence, [California,] is returning to publishing weekly after three months as a daily due to declining advertising. *Ming Pao Daily* in New York will shut down entirely, while *Hoy New York* abandoned print at the end of last year [2008]. At the venerable *Ebony* and *Jet* in Chicago, all employees must reapply for their jobs—that is, the jobs that remain.

With the ever-deepening cuts across the news business, these losses may seem worth no more than a shrug. *Asian-*

Sally Lehrman, "The Danger of Losing the Ethnic Media," *Boston Globe*, March 5, 2009. Reprinted with permission.

Week, after all, employs only 11 staffers. But the harm goes deep. Ethnic media play a vital role in the communities they serve and do a great deal of unrecognized work for journalism.

Cultivating Democracy

Ethnic media, like other news media, recognize that an informed populace will help keep government accountable. Armed with knowledge of current events and issues, the public can become wise participants in societal decision-making. Ethnic media also cultivate democracy in ways that the mainstream seems to have abandoned. *Univision*, for instance, has led bipartisan citizenship and voter registration drives during the past two presidential elections. This involvement in the democratic process might appear unseemly to some traditionalists. But at least according to the Society of Professional Journalists Code of Ethics, this is the US news media's fundamental role: to further democracy.

Day after day, the various branches of the ethnic media follow some of the most important and contentious issues, ones that grab the attention of the mainstream only sporadically. Take immigration. A reader might find a story now and then on CNN or the Associated Press. But Impremedia, which owns eight Spanish-language print outlets including *Hoy New York*, features as many as 10 immigration stories on its website every day.

Issues Overlooked by Mainstream Media

Ethnic media can help steer the mainstream away from short-sighted and shallow reporting on communities and the ways in which race and ethnicity operate in all of our lives. When the *New Yorker* and National Public Radio's Daniel Schorr declared that Barack Obama's campaign signaled a new "post-racial" era, the rest of the mainstream took up the theme. We do all get along, the story went, and Obama's success proved it. The black media, however, were quick to point out that one black president might create dramatic change, but could not transform a history of institutionalized inequities.

Ethnic media, like other news media, recognize that an informed populace will help keep government accountable.

When the *New Yorker* ran its infamous caricature of Barack and Michelle Obama, the mainstream news interviewed comedians who worried about making fun of a black president. But Eric Easter of *Ebony/Jet* offered more insight. He wrote about the powerful impact of grotesque, racialized cartoons, from political propaganda of the Nazi era to family fare of recent decades, that "still find their ways . . . into the backs of our minds." The *New Yorker* cover did not affront because the joke failed, but because it harkened back to the dehumanizing imagery that takes up residence in our reactive minds.

Ethnic media see their role as primarily to give voice to the community, strengthen cohesion, and chronicle community life. They also consider it important to correct misperceptions promulgated by the rest of the news. They report about the community from the inside out, sometimes quite literally. When inmates of the Reeves County Detention Center protested poor medical care at the privately run Texas facility, most outlets highlighted the damage to buildings. Telemundo's station in Midland/Odessa, Texas, also described the plight of hundreds of inmates—detained there on immigration violations—who slept outside in makeshift tents despite the freezing weather.

More than 42 percent of print newsrooms across the country employ no black, Asian American, Latino, or American Indian journalists at all. According to even the most generous analyses, they consult white sources at least two-thirds of the time. With their ability to tap into the communities they serve, the ethnic media contribute context, history, and per-spectives found nowhere else.

12

New Media Underscore the Challenges of Journalistic Gatekeeping

Kendyl Salcito

Kendyl Salcito has a master's degree in journalism and is the executive director of Nomogaia, an organization that focuses on global human rights.

Those who are in control of news guard the gates of information. Traditional news media have long been the gatekeepers, who—at their best—provide factual, balanced journalism. New media platforms are weakening these gates to the point where news can be unreliable. In countries without a free press, the government acts as the gatekeeper, ensuring that people only get the official version of the news. In such cases, gatekeeping is too strong, and new media can bring in perspectives that increase discourse and democracy. Ultimately, the advent of the Internet may have heralded a time with so much available information that the public will become the gatekeepers.

Journalists have long considered themselves the gatekeepers of news and information for the public. Indeed, whether self-imposed or not, some form of gatekeeping seems unavoidable in journalism. In any newspaper, magazine, or news broadcast, an editor judges which stories are appropriate, which sources are credible, which quotes are valuable, and so on.

Kendyl Salcito, "Gatekeeping," *School of Journalism and Mass Communication, University of Wisconsin-Madison*, 2009. Reprinted with permission.

Gatekeeping in early journalism history was not considered a serious editorial problem, because it was assumed that almost anyone could operate a press and express views. When presses became expensive and moguls created major news organizations, the problem of gatekeeping arose.

History of Gatekeeping

Gatekeeping—as a system of rules, editorial checks and other verificational processes—became important to journalism ethics with the rise of the modern newspaper in the late 19th century, when papers advertised claims of their objectivity and factuality in news reporting. In this context, gatekeeping became a norm of responsible reporting, where editors and journalists checked their reports for facts and balance. Only by the mid-1900s, when concerns arose about media power and concentration, did analysts begin to see gatekeeping as potentially harmful to journalism and to democracy.

With the advent of the internet, has information flow been freed from the gatekeepers of mainstream news media? Or has news become compromised, barely distinguishable from rumor and gossip? The news media's gatekeeping role used to dictate the newsworthiness of an event—in terms of its importance and also its validity. The rise of the internet has, to resort to an often-used metaphor, left gate keepers guarding their gates while the rest of the wall crumbles away. Since the news media can no longer monitor what does and does not reach the public sphere, the task of gatekeeping has become more methodological and analytical, stressing the verification of facts and the reliability of sources.

The fundamental ethical problems stem from both the existence of gatekeeping mechanisms and the deterioration thereof. These problems are perhaps best exemplified in two case studies. The first, a case of excessive media gatekeeping, arises in Myanmar (formerly Burma). The other, a case of disenfranchised gatekeepers, arises in the United States. The relative powerlessness of North American gatekeepers engenders the risk that news media may lack authority even to counteract false rumors spread in the blogosphere and on partisan websites.

With the advent of the internet, has information flow been freed from the gatekeepers of mainstream news media?

Burma: Gatekeeping at Its Strongest

The Burmese news media consists almost entirely of government-sponsored (and censored) publications and broadcasts. Editors-censors rid international articles of any 'unwanted' information before printing or airing them. Burmese journalists have learned to self-censor rather than risk harsh punishment and firing. The result is a media of one gate, rigorously guarded. There are no bloggers in Myanmar, as internet use is restricted to government-monitored non-web email and a few token websites approved by the government. Yahoo, Google, and NYTimes.com are unknown entities in Myanmar.

The system is highly effective for the information-disseminators, because the precise message they hope to relay to the public is in fact relayed impeccably (though not always credibly). Obviously, however, this micromanagement severely hampers a free press.

Recently, a Burmese expatriate refugee group (The Democratic Voice of Burma [DVB]) based in Europe began broadcasting a Burmese-language television and radio show from Norway into Myanmar. Though DVB is in its own right a gatekeeper, submitting only its pre-selected information to the airwaves, the new gate it created provides an alternate viewpoint from the government-supported broadcasts. Destruction (albeit partial) of the gatekeeping mechanism is providing a portion of the Burmese population with the means and mindset for discourse.

In this extreme example of gatekeeping, it is clear that when the gates are breached, diverse ideas and discussions can arise. Some analysts feel that democracy can be empowered as gatekeepers fade away. As more voices fill the public sphere, replacing the old—and few—voices of authority, the diversity of popular opinion becomes the new basis for thought and analysis. In that regard, it may seem that the role of gatekeeper is obsolete and should be eradicated. But recent events in the United States, such as those during the 2004 presidential election, suggest that gatekeeping is still important, in some forms.

Enabling viewers to become their own gatekeepers in broadcast journalism could have positive and/or negative results.

The USA: Gatekeeping at Its Weakest?

A number of incidents in the United States exemplify the risks of a media without gatekeepers. Bill Kovach and Tom Rosentiel, in their book *Warp Speed*, used the Monica Lewinsky affair to illustrate the shift in news gatekeeping in the internet age. Within the first chapter, Rosentiel and Kovach assert that the unverified reporting on President [Bill Clinton's] sexual affair with the White House intern showed that "there are no more gatekeepers." Anything is publishable because anyone can publish a blog. Taken a step further, as political author James B. Stuart does, the gatekeepers are those who, "armed with the technology of the internet," produce their stories with extraordinary speed, without "filtering information on grounds of taste, relevance, or accuracy." In 2004, the consequences of weak gatekeeping were evident in a rumor, spread by Matt Drudge, that the Democratic presidential candidate, John Kerry, had an affair with a female journalist. *The Wall Street Journal*, the British tabloid *The Sun* and the *National Review* (not to mention countless bloggers) took the Kerry rumor at face value, spreading it, unsubstantiated, among their readers. However, to their credit, several mainstream media outlets adhered to their journalistic principles and ignored the story until Alexandra Polier, the alleged "other woman," denied the rumor.

Not all journalists continue to adhere to the role and standards of gatekeeper. Hard evidence is sometimes hard to come by, and some journalists have shirked their journalistic responsibilities to build a story where facts are scarce. Some of the U.S. news coverage in the wake of the Katrina hurricane of 2005 exemplifies this failure. According to Henry W. Fischer III, the Director of the Center for Disaster Research and Education at Millersville University in Pennsylvania: "The bigger and more diffuse the disaster, the more the gatekeeping function of the media fails in the rush to get the story out." Katrina coverage was rife with rumor and wild death-toll estimates, many of which originated in online accounts provided by bloggers.

Keeping the Media in Check

However, bloggers and citizen-journalists are in a position to improve the quality of news and criticize the news media for shortfalls in their information-gathering and reporting. They help circulate information that the mainstream media could miss. Such was the case in the wake of the assassination of Dutch politician Pim Fortuyn in May 2002. The traditional news media labeled Fortuyn "anti-Muslim," "hard right wing," and "the Dutch [equivalent of France's fascist candidate] Jean Marie Le Pen" even as they called his assassination a tragedy. The harsh labels overlooked Fortuyn's actual political platform, though. Web writers (particularly Adam Curry [at] www.curry.com) brought a valuable alternative perspective to light, describing the much more complicated issues that Fortuyn addressed, including deep concern for Muslim women's rights, apprehension about the open-minded nature of Dutch society (he was gay) in the face of a hugely conservative Islamic influx, and a basic culture clash. Curry's blog explained that Fortuyn "never called for a 'Ban on immigration' or 'Removal of Muslims'. . . . What Pim did do, was start the public debate about immigration and the standard of living in the Netherlands, which is the second most densely populated country in the world." Whether one agrees with Curry or not, bloggers like him can provide more information and perspective on news and issues.

Novel Uses of Gatekeeping

Journalist-bloggers lend credibility to their online discourses by providing links to websites containing their raw data and references (e.g. a Gallup poll cited in an article will include a hyperlink to the poll results). At the same time, they frequently add hyperlinks that send readers to the top US daily newspapers and news agencies such as the *New York Times, Washington Post, Boston Globe,* and the Associated Press, thus almost re-evoking the gatekeepers.

Gatekeeping has taken on an intriguing new shape in the form of Britain's new Channel 4 online news shows. Beginning in October, 2005, Channel 4 [started] broadcasting soft news shows strictly online. The topics thus far are special-interest (cars, fashion, technology and the like), so their news value is limited at this point. The novelty is the format: the shows are in chapter format, so viewers can pick and choose what they want to watch. Enabling viewers to become their own gatekeepers in broadcast journalism could have positive and/or negative results. Possibly the public gatekeeping will enable news broadcasters to broaden their sphere of coverage and target a wider audience. Equally probable, however, [is that] online broadcasters could opt to cut the less-visited news chapters on their online shows, thus limiting the scope of broadcast news.

Organizations to Contact

The editors have compiled the following list of organizations concerned with the issues debated in this book. The descriptions are derived from materials provided by the organizations. All have publications or information available for interested readers. The list was compiled on the date of publication of the present volume; street and online addresses may change. Be aware that many organizations take several weeks or longer to respond to inquiries, so allow as much time as possible.

American Press Institute (API)
11690 Sunrise Valley Dr., Reston, VA   20191
(703) 620-3611 • fax: (703) 620-5814
e-mail: info@americanpressinstitute.org
website: www.americanpressinstitute.org

Founded by newspaper publishers in 1946, the American Press Institute (API) is devoted solely to the training and professional development of the news industry and journalism educators. The institute conducts seminars for journalists, sales, marketing, and management professionals in print, broadcast, cable, and digital media companies. In 2006, API launched Newspaper Next, a research initiative designed to explore new business models and promote innovative sustainable growth in the news industry.

American Society of News Editors (ASNE)
11690B Sunrise Valley Dr., Reston, VA   20191
(703) 453-1122
website: www.asne.org

The American Society of News Editors (ASNE), founded in 1922 as a nonprofit professional organization, focuses on leadership development and journalism-related issues. ASNE aims to promote fair and principled journalism, defend and protect

First Amendment rights, and fight for freedom of information and open government. It is committed to fostering the public discourse essential to democracy; helping editors to maintain the highest standards of quality, improve their craft, and better serve their communities; and to preserving and promoting core journalistic values while embracing and exploring change. Its website offers various webinars and publications, some of which are available for free.

Free Press

40 Main St., Ste 301, Florence, MA   01062
(877) 888-1533 • fax: (413) 585-8409
e-mail: info@freepress.net
website: www.freepress.net

Launched in 2002, Free Press is a national nonprofit organization that works to reform the media. Through education advocacy and organizing, it promotes diverse and independent media ownership, strong public media, quality journalism, and universal access to communications. It produces the semi-annual newsletter *Media Reform News*, a monthly newsletter, an e-newsletter, and a weekly podcast titled *Media Minutes: (Un) Covering the Media*. A proponent of government involvement in the news industry, the organization also maintains the website SaveTheNews.org, a campaign for government policies that support journalism and a free press.

New Media Consortium (NMC)

6101 W. Courtyard Dr., Bldg. 1, Ste. 100, Austin, TX   78730
(512) 445-4200 • fax: (512) 445-4205
website: www.nmc.org

Founded in 1993, the New Media Consortium (NMC) is an international nonprofit consortium of learning-focused organizations dedicated to the exploration and use of new media and new technologies. Its hundreds of member institutions include colleges and universities, museums, research centers, and businesses. The annual *Horizon Report* describes the continuing work of the NMC's Horizon Project, a research-oriented effort that seeks to identify and describe emerging technologies likely to have considerable impact on teaching, learning, and creative expression within higher education.

Newspaper Association of America (NAA)

4401 Wilson Blvd., Ste. 900, Arlington, VA   22203-1867
(571) 366-1000 • fax: (571) 366-1195
e-mail: info@naa.org
website: www.naa.org

The Newspaper Association of America (NAA) is a nonprofit organization representing nearly two thousand newspapers and their multiplatform businesses in the United States and Canada. NAA members include daily newspapers as well as non-dailies, other print publications, and online products. The association focuses on the major issues that affect today's newspaper industry: public policy/legal matters, advertising revenue growth, and audience development across the media's broad portfolio of products and digital platforms. The NAA website houses an extensive library of resources related to all aspects of newspaper media. The collection includes articles, reports, presentations, books, and audio clips.

The Poynter Institute

801 Third St. South, St. Petersburg, FL   33701
(727) 821-9494 • fax: (727) 553-4680
e-mail: seminars@poyntner.org
website: www.poyntner.org

Founded in 1975, the Poynter Institute is dedicated to all aspects of journalism. It functions as a school for journalism and a resource for news business logistics and leadership. Through its website, the institute issues the newsletters *Media Lab, Business News*, and *Making Sense of News*. It also publishes the blog *Romanesko*, popular among industry professionals for its news leads, commentary, and insider information.

The Reporters Committee for Freedom of the Press
1101 Wilson Blvd., Ste. 1100, Arlington, VA   22209
(800) 336-4243 • fax: (703) 807-2109
e-mail: rcfp@rcfp.org
website: www.rcfp.org

The Reporters Committee for Freedom of the Press was created in 1970 following a wave of government subpoenas asking reporters to name confidential sources. Since then, it has
consistently played a role in freedom of the press cases that
have come before the US Supreme Court. The committee acts
as a resource for free-speech issues through its quarterly legal
review, a weekly newsletter, a twenty-four-hour hotline, and
various handbooks on media-law issues. The committee continues to advocate for reporters' interests, particularly in the
face of new challenges posed by digital platforms.

Bibliography

Books

Dan Barry   *Pull Me Up: A Memoir*. New York:
                        Norton, 2004.

Bart Camaerts   *Reclaiming the Media:*
and Nico   *Communication Rights and*
Carpentier   *Democratic Media Roles*. Chicago:
                        University of Chicago Press, 2007.

Timothy E. Cook   *Governing with the News*. 2nd ed. *The*
                        News Media as a Political Institution.
                        Chicago: University of Chicago Press,
                        2005.

Paul Gillin   *The New Influencers: A Marketer's*
                        Guide to the New Social Media.
                        Sanger, CA: Quill Driver Books/Word
                        Dancer Press, 2007.

Dan Gillmor   *We the Media: Grassroots Journalism*
                        by the People for the People.
                        Sebastopol, CA: O'Reilly Media,
                        2006.

Hugh Hewitt   *Blog: Understanding the Information*
                        Reformation That's Changing Your
                        World. Nashville: Thomas Nelson,
                        Inc., 2005.

Bill Kovach and Tom Rosenstiel	*The Elements of Journalism: What Newspaper People Should Know and the Public Should Expect.* Rev. and updated. New York: Three Rivers Press, 2007.
Robert McChesney and John Nichols	*The Death and Life of American Journalism: The Media Revolution That Will Begin the World Again.* Philadelphia: Nation Books, 2010.
Philip Meyer	*The Vanishing Newspaper: Saving Journalism in the Information Age.* Updated 2nd ed. Columbia: University of Missouri Press, 2004.
Bill Moggridge	*Designing Media.* Cambridge, MA: MIT Press, 2010.
Alexander Osterwalder	*Business Model Generation: A Handbook for Visionaries, Game Changers, and Challengers.* Hoboken, NJ: John Wiley, 2010.
Mary Jane Pardue	*Who Owns the Press? Investigating Public vs. Private Ownership of America's Newspapers.* Portland, OR: Marion Street Press, 2010.

Periodicals

| Eric Alterman | "Out of Print: The Death and Life of the American Newspaper," *New Yorker*, March 31, 2008. |
| Chris Anderson and Michael Wolff | "The Web Is Dead. Long Live the Internet," *Wired*, August, 2010. |

Sewell Chan   "Panel Discussion: New Media, Old Media and Advocacy," *New York Times*, September 5, 2007.

Randy Dotinga   "Nonprofit Journalism on the Rise," *Christian Science Monitor*, February 12, 2008.

Claudia Eller   "Jeff Sagansky Stakes Claim to New Media Future," *Los Angeles Times*, July 29, 2010.

Paul Farhi   "A Costly Mistake? When the Associated Press Decided a Decade Ago to Sell Its News Content to Online Portals, It May Have Hastened the Decline of the Daily Newspapers That Own the Wire Service," *American Journalism Review*, April–May 2009.

A.G. Gancarski   "Death Throes: The Demise of Sports Journalism," *American Conservative*, November 1, 2009.

Robert Giles   "New Economic Models for Journalism," *Daedalus*, March 22, 2010.

Gabrielle Gurley   "The Herald's Head Man: Q&A with Joe Sciacca, Editor in Chief," *Commonwealth*, November 10, 2010.

Michael Hirschhorn   "End Times: Can America's Paper of Record Survive the Death of Newsprint? Can Journalism?" *Atlantic*, January/February 2009.

Howard Kurtz   "The Death of Print?" *Washington Post*, May 11, 2009.

John Nichols   "David Simon, Arianna Huffington and the Future of Journalism," *Nation*, May 25, 2009.

Barb Palser   "Investing in the Future," *American Journalism Review*, December/January 2009.

Kevin Poulsen   "Lieberman Introduces Anti-Wikileaks Legislation," *Wired*, December 2, 2010.

Gillian Reagan   "Paywall or Not, a Renewed Focus on Digital at the *Times*," *New York Observer*, October 21, 2009.

Alan Rusbridger   "The Splintering of the Fourth Estate," *Guardian* (Manchester, UK), November 19, 2010.

Charu Lata Singh   "New Media and Cultural Identity," *China Media Research*, January 2010.

Edward Wasserman   "Government Can't Fix News Business," *Miami Herald*, June 2, 2010.

Index